SERMON NOTES WRITTEN BY

_____

BEGINNING ON

_____

WEEKLY SERMON NOTES

JOURNAL

Ink & Willow

CONTENTS

BOOKS OF THE BIBLE

OLD TESTAMENT

Genesis	2 Chronicles	Daniel
Exodus	Ezra	Hosea
Leviticus	Nehemiah	Joel
Numbers	Esther	Amos
Deuteronomy	Job	Obadiah
Joshua	Psalms	Jonah
Judges	Proverbs	Micah
Ruth	Ecclesiastes	Nahum
1 Samuel	Song of Solomon	Habakkuk
2 Samuel	Isaiah	Zephaniah
1 Kings	Jeremiah	Haggai
2 Kings	Lamentations	Zechariah
1 Chronicles	Ezekiel	Malachi

NEW TESTAMENT

Matthew	Ephesians	Hebrews
Mark	Philippians	James
Luke	Colossians	1 Peter
John	1 Thessalonians	2 Peter
Acts	2 Thessalonians	1 John
Romans	1 Timothy	2 John
1 Corinthians	2 Timothy	3 John
2 Corinthians	Titus	Jude
Galatians	Philemon	Revelation

NAMES FOR GOD

Adonai
LORD

El Elyon
GOD MOST HIGH

El Shaddai
GOD ALMIGHTY

Abba
FATHER

I AM

Jehovah Raah
THE LORD
MY SHEPHERD

Jehovah Rapha
THE GOD
WHO HEALS

Yahweh

Jehovah Nissi
THE LORD
MY BANNER

Jehovah Jireh
THE LORD
MY PROVIDER

El Roi
THE GOD
WHO SEES

El Olam
ETERNAL GOD

HEBREW WORDS OF NOTE

Amen (Revelation 22:21) **"so be it"**	truth and confirmation
Emunah (Hebrews 11:1) **"faith; belief"**	the assurance of things hoped for; a faith that leads to faithfulness in action
Hesed/Chesed (Isaiah 54:10) **"love; lovingkindness"**	unfailing, unconditional, loyal love put into action
Hineni (Genesis 22:1) **"Here I am."**	expression of complete availability and readiness in response to God's call
Nephesh (Genesis 2:7) **"soul; life"**	desires, heart, or appetite
Qadosh (Psalm 96:9) **"holy"**	set apart for a special purpose
Ruach (Isaiah 59:19) **"spirit; breath"**	a holy rushing tide or wind
Shalom (Judges 6:24) **"peace"**	perfection in God; wholeness, completeness, soundness, harmony
Shema (Deuteronomy 6:4) **"hear"**	a hearing that requires action; that is, to hear God also means to obey God
Teshuva (Joel 2:12) **"returning to God; repentance"**	a total turning away from one direction and intentional movement or return toward God
Tikvah (Jeremiah 29:11) **"hope"**	expectation, strong faith; a rock to hold fast to
Tov (Genesis 1:31) **"good"**	like a fine-tuned machine; functional; capable of fulfilling a God-given purpose
Yirah (Proverbs 9:10) **"awe; fear"**	a speechless awe that leads to respect, reverence, and worship

DATE _____ ● _____

SERMON TITLE _____

SPEAKER _____

LOCATION _____

KEY SCRIPTURES _____

_____

_____

NOTES

DATE _____ ● _____

SERMON TITLE _____

SPEAKER _____

LOCATION _____

KEY SCRIPTURES _____

_____

_____

NOTES

DATE _____ ◆ _____

SERMON TITLE _____

SPEAKER _____

LOCATION _____

KEY SCRIPTURES _____

_____

_____

NOTES

DATE _____ ♦ _____

SERMON TITLE _____

SPEAKER _____

LOCATION _____

KEY SCRIPTURES _____

_____

_____

NOTES

DATE _____ ◉ _____

SERMON TITLE _____

SPEAKER _____

LOCATION _____

KEY SCRIPTURES _____

_____

_____

NOTES

DATE _____ ● _____

SERMON TITLE _____

SPEAKER _____ _____

LOCATION _____

KEY SCRIPTURES _____

_____

_____

NOTES

DATE _____ ● _____

SERMON TITLE _____

SPEAKER _____ _____

LOCATION _____

KEY SCRIPTURES _____

_____

_____

NOTES

DATE _____

SERMON TITLE _____

SPEAKER _____

LOCATION _____

KEY SCRIPTURES _____

NOTES

DATE _____ ◆ _____

SERMON TITLE _____

SPEAKER _____

LOCATION _____

KEY SCRIPTURES _____

_____

_____

NOTES

DATE _____

SERMON TITLE _____

SPEAKER _____

LOCATION _____

KEY SCRIPTURES _____

NOTES

DATE _____ 🔷 _____

SERMON TITLE _____

SPEAKER _____

LOCATION _____

KEY SCRIPTURES _____

_____

_____

NOTES

DATE _____ ● _____

SERMON TITLE _____

SPEAKER _____   _____

LOCATION _____

KEY SCRIPTURES _____

_____

_____

NOTES

DATE _____ ● _____

SERMON TITLE _____

SPEAKER _____

LOCATION _____

KEY SCRIPTURES _____

_____

_____

NOTES

DATE _____ ◆ _____

SERMON TITLE _____

SPEAKER _____ _____

LOCATION _____

KEY SCRIPTURES _____

_____

_____

NOTES

DATE _____ ● _____

SERMON TITLE _____

SPEAKER ___ _____

LOCATION _____

KEY SCRIPTURES _____
_____
_____

NOTES

DATE _____ ● _____

SERMON TITLE _____

SPEAKER _____

LOCATION _____

KEY SCRIPTURES _____

_____

_____

NOTES

DATE _____ ● _____

SERMON TITLE _____

SPEAKER _____ _____

LOCATION _____

KEY SCRIPTURES _____

_____

_____

NOTES

DATE _____ ◆ _____

SERMON TITLE _____

SPEAKER _____ _____

LOCATION _____

KEY SCRIPTURES _____

_____

_____

NOTES

DATE _____ ◆ _____

SERMON TITLE _____

SPEAKER _____

LOCATION _____

KEY SCRIPTURES _____

_____

_____

NOTES

DATE _____ 🌢 _____

SERMON TITLE _____

SPEAKER _____ _____

LOCATION _____

KEY SCRIPTURES _____

_____

_____

NOTES

DATE _____ ● _____

SERMON TITLE _____

SPEAKER _____   _____

LOCATION _____

KEY SCRIPTURES _____

_____

_____

NOTES

DATE _____ ● _____

SERMON TITLE _____

SPEAKER _____

LOCATION _____

KEY SCRIPTURES _____

_____

_____

NOTES

DATE _____ ● _____

SERMON TITLE _____

SPEAKER _____ _____

LOCATION _____

KEY SCRIPTURES _____

_____

_____

NOTES

DATE _____ ◆ _____

SERMON TITLE _____

SPEAKER _____

LOCATION _____

KEY SCRIPTURES _____

_____

_____

NOTES

DATE _____ ● _____

SERMON TITLE _____

SPEAKER _____

LOCATION _____

KEY SCRIPTURES _____

_____

_____

NOTES

DATE _____ ◆ _____

SERMON TITLE _____

SPEAKER _____

LOCATION _____

KEY SCRIPTURES _____

_____

_____

NOTES

DATE _____ ● _____

SERMON TITLE _____

SPEAKER _____

LOCATION _____

KEY SCRIPTURES _____

_____

_____

NOTES

DATE _____ 🖤 _____

SERMON TITLE _____

SPEAKER _____

LOCATION _____

KEY SCRIPTURES _____

_____

_____

NOTES

DATE _____ ● _____

SERMON TITLE _____

SPEAKER _____

LOCATION _____

KEY SCRIPTURES _____

_____

_____

NOTES

DATE _____ • _____

SERMON TITLE _____

SPEAKER _____

LOCATION _____

KEY SCRIPTURES _____

_____

_____

NOTES

DATE _____ ⬩ _____

SERMON TITLE _____

SPEAKER _____

LOCATION _____

KEY SCRIPTURES _____

_____

_____

NOTES

DATE _____ ● _____

SERMON TITLE _____

SPEAKER _____

LOCATION _____

KEY SCRIPTURES _____

_____

_____

NOTES

DATE _____ ♦ _____

SERMON TITLE _____

SPEAKER _____

LOCATION _____

KEY SCRIPTURES _____

_____

_____

NOTES

DATE _____ ♦ _____

SERMON TITLE _____

SPEAKER _____

LOCATION _____

KEY SCRIPTURES _____

_____

_____

NOTES

DATE _____ ● _____

SERMON TITLE _____

SPEAKER _____

LOCATION _____

KEY SCRIPTURES _____

_____

_____

NOTES

DATE _____ ◆ _____

SERMON TITLE _____

SPEAKER _____

LOCATION _____

KEY SCRIPTURES _____

_____

_____

NOTES

DATE _____ ● _____

SERMON TITLE _____

SPEAKER _____

LOCATION _____

KEY SCRIPTURES _____

_____

_____

NOTES

DATE _____ ⚬ _____

SERMON TITLE _____

SPEAKER _____

LOCATION _____

KEY SCRIPTURES _____

_____

_____

NOTES

DATE _____ ⦿ _____

SERMON TITLE _____

SPEAKER _____

LOCATION _____

KEY SCRIPTURES _____

_____

_____

NOTES

DATE _____ ● _____

SERMON TITLE _____

SPEAKER _____

LOCATION _____

KEY SCRIPTURES _____

_____

_____

NOTES

DATE _____ ● _____

SERMON TITLE _____

SPEAKER _____

LOCATION _____

KEY SCRIPTURES _____

_____

_____

NOTES

DATE _____ ● _____

SERMON TITLE _____

SPEAKER _____

LOCATION _____

KEY SCRIPTURES _____

_____

_____

NOTES

DATE _____ ⬤ _____

SERMON TITLE _____

SPEAKER _____

LOCATION _____

KEY SCRIPTURES _____

_____

_____

NOTES

DATE _____ ● _____

SERMON TITLE _____

SPEAKER _____

LOCATION _____

KEY SCRIPTURES _____

_____

_____

NOTES

DATE _____ ● _____

SERMON TITLE _____

SPEAKER _____

LOCATION _____

KEY SCRIPTURES _____

_____

_____

NOTES

DATE _____ ♦ _____

SERMON TITLE _____

SPEAKER _____

LOCATION _____

KEY SCRIPTURES _____

_____

_____

NOTES

DATE _____ ❦ _____

SERMON TITLE _____

SPEAKER _____

LOCATION _____

KEY SCRIPTURES _____

_____

_____

NOTES

DATE _____ 🔔 _____

SERMON TITLE _____

SPEAKER _____

LOCATION _____

KEY SCRIPTURES _____

_____

_____

NOTES

DATE _____ ◆ _____

SERMON TITLE _____

SPEAKER _____

LOCATION _____

KEY SCRIPTURES _____

_____

_____

NOTES

DATE _____ ● _____

SERMON TITLE _____

SPEAKER _____

LOCATION _____

KEY SCRIPTURES _____

_____

_____

NOTES

DATE _____ ● _____

SERMON TITLE _____

SPEAKER _____

LOCATION _____

KEY SCRIPTURES _____

_____

_____

NOTES

DATE _____ ● _____

SERMON TITLE _____

SPEAKER _____

LOCATION _____

KEY SCRIPTURES _____

_____

_____

NOTES

DATE _____ ● _____

SERMON TITLE _____

SPEAKER _____

LOCATION _____

KEY SCRIPTURES _____

_____

_____

NOTES

DATE _____  _____

SERMON TITLE _____

SPEAKER _____

LOCATION _____

KEY SCRIPTURES _____

_____

_____

NOTES

DATE _____ ● _____

SERMON TITLE _____

SPEAKER _____

LOCATION _____

KEY SCRIPTURES _____

_____

_____

NOTES

DATE _____ ● _____

SERMON TITLE _____

SPEAKER _____

LOCATION _____

KEY SCRIPTURES _____

_____

_____

NOTES

DATE _____ ♦ _____

SERMON TITLE _____

SPEAKER _____

LOCATION _____

KEY SCRIPTURES _____

_____

_____

NOTES

DATE _____ ● _____

SERMON TITLE _____

SPEAKER _____

LOCATION _____

KEY SCRIPTURES _____

_____

_____

NOTES

DATE _____ ● _____

SERMON TITLE _____

SPEAKER _____

LOCATION _____

KEY SCRIPTURES _____

_____

_____

NOTES

DATE _____ ◆ _____

SERMON TITLE _____

SPEAKER _____

LOCATION _____

KEY SCRIPTURES _____
_____
_____

NOTES

DATE _____ ⦿ _____

SERMON TITLE _____

SPEAKER _____

LOCATION _____

KEY SCRIPTURES _____

_____

_____

NOTES

DATE _____ ● _____

SERMON TITLE _____

SPEAKER _____

LOCATION _____

KEY SCRIPTURES _____

_____

_____

NOTES

DATE _____ ● _____

SERMON TITLE _____

SPEAKER _____

LOCATION _____

KEY SCRIPTURES _____

_____

_____

NOTES

DATE _____ 🔔 _____

SERMON TITLE _____

SPEAKER _____

LOCATION _____

KEY SCRIPTURES _____

_____

_____

NOTES

DATE _____ ●_____

SERMON TITLE _____

SPEAKER _____

LOCATION _____

KEY SCRIPTURES _____

_____

_____

NOTES

DATE _____ ● _____

SERMON TITLE _____

SPEAKER _____

LOCATION _____

KEY SCRIPTURES _____

_____

_____

NOTES

DATE _____ ● _____

SERMON TITLE _____

SPEAKER _____

LOCATION _____

KEY SCRIPTURES _____

_____

_____

NOTES

DATE _____ ◗ _____

SERMON TITLE _____

SPEAKER _____

LOCATION _____

KEY SCRIPTURES _____

_____

_____

NOTES

DATE _____ ● _____

SERMON TITLE _____

SPEAKER _____

LOCATION _____

KEY SCRIPTURES _____

_____

_____

NOTES

DATE _____ ◆ _____

SERMON TITLE _____

SPEAKER _____

LOCATION _____

KEY SCRIPTURES _____

_____

_____

NOTES

DATE _____ ● _____

SERMON TITLE _____

SPEAKER _____

LOCATION _____

KEY SCRIPTURES _____

_____

_____

NOTES

DATE _____ ● _____

SERMON TITLE _____

SPEAKER _____

LOCATION _____

KEY SCRIPTURES _____

_____

_____

NOTES

DATE _____ ◆ _____

SERMON TITLE _____

SPEAKER _____

LOCATION _____

KEY SCRIPTURES _____

_____

_____

NOTES

DATE _____ 🔖 _____

SERMON TITLE _____

SPEAKER _____

LOCATION _____

KEY SCRIPTURES _____

_____

_____

NOTES

Prayer Requests

DATE	PRAYER REQUEST	HOW PRAYER WAS ANSWERED

DATE	PRAYER REQUEST	HOW PRAYER WAS ANSWERED

Prayer Requests

DATE	PRAYER REQUEST	HOW PRAYER WAS ANSWERED

DATE	PRAYER REQUEST	HOW PRAYER WAS ANSWERED

Prayer Requests

DATE	PRAYER REQUEST	HOW PRAYER WAS ANSWERED

DATE	PRAYER REQUEST	HOW PRAYER WAS ANSWERED

Prayer Requests

DATE	PRAYER REQUEST	HOW PRAYER WAS ANSWERED

DATE	PRAYER REQUEST	HOW PRAYER WAS ANSWERED

Announcements

*Record any church announcements, upcoming event details,
baby dedications, baptisms, or other important dates.*

Announcements

Announcements

Recommended Reading

*List any books, articles, or other sources mentioned in
a sermon that you would like to check out later.*

○ _____

○ _____

○ _____

○ _____

○ _____

○ _____

○ _____

○ _____

○ _____

○ _____

○ _____

○ _____

Recommended Reading

- ○ _____
- ○ _____
- ○ _____
- ○ _____
- ○ _____
- ○ _____
- ○ _____
- ○ _____
- ○ _____
- ○ _____
- ○ _____
- ○ _____
- ○ _____

Recommended Reading

○ _____

○ _____

○ _____

○ _____

○ _____

○ _____

○ _____

○ _____

○ _____

○ _____

○ _____

○ _____

○ _____

SOURCES

Avital Snow, "Here Am I!—the Hebrew Meaning of Hineni,"
FIRM (Fellowship of Israel Related Ministries), October 19, 2021,
https://firmisrael.org/learn/here-am-i-the-hebrew-meaning-of-hineni.

Clarence L. Haynes Jr., "10 Hebrew Words from the Bible That
Every Christian Should Know," Crosswalk.com, November 29, 2021,
www.crosswalk.com/faith/bible-study/hebrew-words-from-the-bible-
that-every-christian-should-know.html.

Esther Wieja, "Hebrew Words Every Christian Should Know:
A Glossary," FIRM (Fellowship of Israel Related Ministries), May 7,
2024, https://firmisrael.org/learn/hebrew-words-every-christian-
should-know-a-glossary.

Estera Wieja, "Start Learning Hebrew with These Important Words,"
FIRM (Fellowship of Israel Related Ministries), October 7, 2021,
https://firmisrael.org/learn/start-learning-hebrew-with-these-
important-words.

Hebrew Roots Mom, "9 Hebrew Words to Bring You Closer to God,"
Holy Branches, accessed June 5, 2024, https://hebrewrootsmom.
com/9-hebrew-words-to-bring-you-closer-to-god.

One Covenant, "Tov—A Word Study," RYM Covenant, June 13, 2021,
https://rymcovenant.net/tov-a-word-study.

An I⎰ ⎰ de Paperback Original

Copyrig   ⎰guin Random House LLC

Ink & Willow and colophon are registered trademarks of
Penguin Random House LLC.

Trade Paperback ISBN 978-0-593-60220-1

Printed in Malaysia

inkandwillow.com

2 4 6 8 9 7 5 3 1

Book and cover design by Zaiah Sampson
Cover art: shutterstock.com: Dmitr1ch, cloth texture

For details on special quantity discounts for bulk purchases,
contact specialmarketscms@penguinrandomhouse.com.